C000062282

WILDLIFE CONTEMPLATIONS

REFLECTIONS ON OUR LIVING WORLD

TRIGGER™
The mental health & wellbeing publisher

Published in Great Britain 2020 by Trigger Publishing

Originally published as The Wildlife Companion in Great Britain

2004 by Robson Books

Trigger is a trading style of Shaw Callaghan Ltd

& Shaw Callaghan 23 USA, INC.

The Foundation Centre

Navigation House, 48 Millgate, Newark

Nottinghamshire NG24 4TS UK

www.triggerpublishing.com

British Library Cataloguing in Publication Data

A CIP catalogue record for this book is available upon request
from the British Library

ISBN: 9781789562033

This book is also available in the following eBook formats:

ePUB: 9781789562040

Cover design by stevewilliamscreative.com

Typeset by stevewilliamscreative.com

Printed and bound in Great Britain by CPI Group (UK) Ltd,
Croydon CR0 4YY

Paper from responsible sources

CONTENTS

NATURE NOTES

O simple Nature, how I do delight
To pause upon thy trifles - foolish things,
As some would call them. On the summer night,
Tracing the lane-path where the dog-rose hings
With dew-drops seeth'd, while chick'ring cricket sings;
My eye can't help but glance upon its leaves,
Where love's warm beauty steals her sweetest blush,
When, soft the while, the Even silent heaves
Her pausing breath just trembling thro' the bush,
And then again dies calm, and all is hush.
O how I feel, just as I pluck the flower
And stick it to my breast - words can't reveal;
But there are souls that in this lovely hour
Know all I mean, and feel whate'er I feel.

JOHN CLARE, Nature

PAUSE FOR THOUGHT

I was born in September, and love it best of all the months. There is no heat, no hurry, no thirst and weariness in corn harvest as there is in the hay. If the season is late, as is usual with us, then mid-September sees the corn still standing in shock. The mornings come slowly. The earth is like a woman married and fading; she does not leap up with a laugh for the first fresh kiss of dawn, but slowly, quietly, unexpectantly likes watching the waking of each new day. The blue mist, like memory in the eyes of a neglected wife, never goes from the wooded hill, and only at noon creeps from the near hedges. There is no bird to put a song in the throat of the morning; only the crow's voice speaks during the day.

Perhaps there is the regular breathing hust of the scythe – even the fretful jar of the mowing machine. But next day, in the morning, all is still again. The lying corn is wet, and when you have bound it, and lift the heavy sheaf to make the stook, the tresses of oats wreathe round each other and droop mournfully.

DH LAWRENCE, The White Peacock, (1911)

To the dull mind nature is leaden; to the illumined mind the whole world burns and sparkles with light.

RALPH WALDO EMERSON, poet and philosopher

POINT OF INTEREST

Teasel is unique in the plant world in the way in which it blooms. Its flowers first appear in a ring around the middle of the head, and spread slowly outwards. As the blooms are fairly short-lived, the new growths outlive the central growths, effectively creating two further rings that move slowly towards the top and bottom of the head. By the time the plant has released all its seeds, it dies leaving behind a tough structure surrounded by stiff, sharp bristles. This makes it the ideal tool for 'teasing' wool, a process practised since Roman times.

The sun, with all those planets revolving around it and dependent on it, can still ripen a bunch of grapes as if it had nothing else in the universe to do.

GALILEO GALILEI, astronomer

PAUSE FOR THOUGHT

The air was wine, the moist earth-smell wine, the lark's song, the wafts from the cowshed at the top of the field, the pant and smoke of a distant train – all were wine – or song, was it? or odour, this unity they all blent into? I had no words then to describe it, that earth-effluence of which I was so conscious; nor, indeed have I found words since. I ran sideways, shouting; I dug glad heels into the squelching soil; I splashed diamond showers from puddles with a stick; I hurled clods skywards at random, and presently I somehow found myself singing. The words were mere nonsense – irresponsible babble; the tune was an improvisation, a weary, unrhythmic thing of rise and fall: and yet it seemed to me a genuine utterance, and just at that moment the one thing fitting and right and perfect. Humanity would have rejected it with scorn. Nature, everywhere singing in the same key, recognised and accepted it without a flicker of dissent.

KENNETH GRAHAME, The Golden Age, (1895)

If one really loves nature, one can find beauty everywhere.

VINCENT VAN GOGH, artist

POINT OF INTEREST

Gossamer is the name given to the light, filmy money-spider webs that appear in grasses on sunny autumn mornings. The name comes from a contraction of goose summer, i.e. St Martin's summer, the feast day in November when geese were once traditionally eaten. The tiny spiders are able to spin their webs across such great distances by allowing themselves to be wafted along on autumn breezes as they spin.

The repetition in nature may not be a mere recurrence. It may be a theatrical 'encore'.

GK CHESTERTON, author

I love Nature partly because she is not man, but a retreat from him. None of his institutions control or pervade her. There a different kind of right prevails. In her midst I can be glad with an entire gladness. If this world were all man, I could not stretch myself, I should lose all hope. He is constraint, she is freedom to me. He makes me wish for another world. She makes me content with this.

HENRY DAVID THOREAU, A Writer's Journal, (1960)

Nature does nothing uselessly.

ARISTOTLE

POINT OF INTEREST

Chaos theory has it that if a butterfly flaps its wings in Tokyo there could be an earthquake in California. But how about if it flaps its wings in America, then magically appears four days later in Cornwall – what does chaos theory have to say about that? The monarch butterfly, one of nature's most astonishing migrants, spends much of life pootling up or down the continent of America, yet occasionally the odd one or two turn up in Britain, the first sighting being in 1876. For years, it was assumed they had stowed away on-board ships – after all, the monarch may be a mighty flyer, but the Atlantic is a far mightier ocean. Yet in 1968 and 1981, the south-west coast of Britain was visited by monarchs in their dozens, at exactly the same time that several species of American birds, true rarities in this country, also turned up. Could the weather be playing a part? Then in 1995, on one day alone in October, at least 45 individual

monarchs were spotted. Unusually, at the end of September that year, three hurricanes had hit the eastern seaboard of the US, resulting in a strong westerly airflow that culminated in a gale in southwestern Britain on September 30. The air flow was reasonably warm, and travelled at around 30-35 knots, taking four days to cross the Atlantic, a short enough time for the butterflies to survive on their fat reserves. It was shown, conclusively, that it was possible for a butterfly to cross the Atlantic aided by nothing but the weather.

I believe in God, only I spell it Nature.

FRANK LLOYD WRIGHT, architect

PAUSE FOR THOUGHT

My own belief is that the natural world cannot be evaluated simply in terms of scientific criteria. Nor can it be dismissed as an arena for the amusement of naturalists. Even broader comparisons - for instance with our heritage of art treasures - can be misleading, and return us to that image of a static museum, a collection of living fossils, from which we have had to argue our way clear. The natural world is ubiquitous; it is too pervasive, too much alive to be contained within any of these models. It touches us all, physically and emotionally, in every aspect of our lives, even when we are not aware of it.

RICHARD MABEY, The Common Ground, (1980)

When one tugs at a single thing in nature, he finds it attached to the rest of the world.

JOHN MUIR, naturalist

POINT OF INTEREST

Anyone who's spent any time in the countryside will have experienced the wrath of the stinging nettle. But what actually is happening to you when the nettle attacks? Each sting is a hollow hair stiffened by silica with a swollen base that contains venom. The tip of this hair is very brittle and when brushed against, no matter how lightly, it breaks off exposing a sharp point that penetrates the skin. It was once thought that the main constituent of the sting was formic acid, the chemical used by ants, but although this acid is present, the main chemicals are histamine, acetylcholine and 5-hydroxytryptamine (serotonin). There is a fourth ingredient that has not yet been identified. Yet while nature takes away with one hand, so it gives with another. Dock, which often grows in the neighbourhood of nettles, contains chemicals in its leaves that neutralise the sting and cool the skin.

Man is the only creature that consumes

without producing.

GEORGE ORWELL, author

It is pleasant to observe any growth in a wood. There is the tract northeast of Beck Stow's Swamp, where some years since I used to go a blackberrying and observed that the pitch pines were beginning to come in; and I have frequently noticed since how fairly they grew, clothing the plain as evenly as if dispersed by art. At first the young pines lined each side of the path like a palisade, they grew so densely, crowding each other to death in this wide world. Eleven years ago I was first aware that I walked in a pitch-pine wood there, and not a blackberry field – which erelong, perchance, I shall survey and lot off for a wood auction, and see the choppers at their work. These trees, I said to myself, are destined for the locomotive's maw; but fortunately it has changed its diet of late, and their branches, which it has taken so many years to mature, are regarded even by the woodman as trash.

HENRY DAVID THOREAU, Faith in a Seed, (1993)

How strange that Nature does not knock,

and yet does not intrude!

EMILY DICKINSON, author

POINT OF INTEREST

Meadow saffron is one of the oldest medicinal plants still in pharmaceutical use today. Its ability to help treat joint pains was recorded as far back as 100 AD, and today its active alkaloid constituent is recognised as a valuable drug, colchicine, for the treatment of acute gout.

ANIMAL WISDOM

Tyger Tyger, burning bright,
In the forests of the night;
What immortal hand or eye,
Could frame thy fearful symmetry?

In what distant deeps or skies.
Burnt the fire of thine eyes?
On what wings dare he aspire?
What the hand, dare seize the fire?

And what shoulder, & what art,
Could twist the sinews of thy heart?
And when thy heart began to beat,
What dread hand? & what dread feet?

What the hammer? what the chain,
In what furnace was thy brain?
What the anvil? what dread grasp,
Dare its deadly terrors clasp!

When the stars threw down their spears
And water'd heaven with their tears:

Did he smile his work to see?
Did he who made the Lamb make thee?

Tyger Tyger burning bright,
In the forests of the night:
What immortal hand or eye,
Dare frame thy fearful symmetry?

WILLIAM BLAKE, The Tyger

On the tenth of April I heard the cuckoo, sitting in Sussex, my back against an oak. A grey mare at grass shared the place with me. Here and hereabout English and Norman had met and fought: there had been din and slaughter. Nothing had changed but men. The oak grew in the same way; the cuckoo came punctually about the second week in April, laid her eggs in other birds' nests and flew away. Yet even that must have had a beginning: there must have been a first time that a cuckoo's two notes broke the quiet of a spring morning, a first time that a cuckoo laid in another bird's nest. Why, among all birds so devoted to their young, should there be this one exception? What a process of mind, you would think, must have replaced instinct, before it could become in its turn instinctive. It is a subterfuge characteristic of the brain of man.

ADRIAN BELL, Men and the Fields, (1939)

The beetle in his hole is a Sultan

ANONYMOUS

POINT OF INTEREST

Moles are mammals, yet they can pursue hugely active lives tunnelling away under the earth where oxygen is not so much thin on the ground, as thin in it. How do they do this? The answer lies in the blood. They have twice as much of it, and twice as much haemoglobin, as other mammals their size. In addition, the haemoglobin has a further enhanced ability when it comes to soaking up whatever oxygen it can find, turning the little creature into a virtual velvet sponge. But moles aren't alone in this adaptation. On the other side of the world, in the high Andean mountains where oxygen is thin in the air, llamas have developed a similarly efficient internal blood system to cope with their environment.

A hippo does not have a sting in its tail,

but a wise man would still rather be sat on

by a bee.

POLISH PROVERB

PAUSE FOR THOUGHT

Everybody is still running towards the Regent's Park, for the purpose of passing half an hour with the Hippopotamus. The animal itself repays public curiosity with a yawn of indifference, or throws cold water on the ardour of his visitors, by suddenly plunging into his bath, and splashing every one within five yards of him. Much disappointment has been expressed at the Hippopotamus, in consequence of its not being exactly up to the general idea of a seahorse, and many hundreds go away grumbling every day, because the brute is not so equestrian in appearance as could be desired. Many persons thought the Hippopotamus was a regular sea-horse, kept expressly for running in harness in a sea-captain's gig; but as the creature turns out to be very like a hog, there are many who go the entire animal in finding fault with him.

PUNCH, December, (1850)

The fox has many tricks. The hedgehog has but one. But that is the best of all.

DESIDERIUS ERASMUS, theologian

POINT OF INTEREST

How do mice, as they scurry about at night, know whether or not they're exploring new areas, or simply scurrying round and round the same spot. According to some recent research, they could be using their own landmarks. Researchers discovered that when woodlice came across an item that differed from most others in an environment, such as, in one experiment, a plastic white disc, it would drag it to the area where it was foraging, then scamper off. After a while, it would return to the disc, then run off in a different direction. It appeared to be using the disc as a landmark to focus its energies more efficiently. Yet plastic white discs are not all that common in the wild, so mice have to make their own landmarks. One common approach is to drag a number of leaves into a small yet distinct pile.

Probably the only British mammal to make a habit of killing and eating adders is the hedgehog, which not only carries a certain immunity to the snake's venom, but also carries at least 6,000 other weapons – its spikes. By poking and prodding at the adder, slipping in little bites when it can, the hedgehog lures the snake into an attack, which it fends off with its spikes. Impaling or wounding itself on the sharp points, the snake steadily weakens, until it is incapable of further attacks or flight. Then the hedgehog pounces, and the battle is over.

Only an owl knows the worth of an owl.

ANONYMOUS

The same evening, under the same beeches on the edge of the wood while the grey slugs came down from the top of the beeches where they spend the day, I saw the wedding of the ants. Those which are to couple have wings and the couples join in the air; but as soon as the male has clasped the female, their wings are entangled, their nerves are agitated, and the two entwined insects turn over and over and fall. The weddings I saw had been exalted very high above the trees, the golden rain fell from leaf to leaf with the sound of a shower, and as each couple touched the ground the two lovers, immediately unjoined, sprang up like the drops of a cascade and flew off rapidly and alone towards the sun and towards death. Strange and almost terrifying vision! I am very proud to have seen the sight and I despise myself for loving with so many precautions, turns and ruses, when I think how the ants give their whole life for life, and only separate for the females to carry the fertilised treasure to the ant-hill and for the males to die. I am inclined to think the males die immediately and that only the females fly up; but I was intoxicated at participating in this mystery, and as soon as I understood it I began to reflect in order to understand it better.

REMY DE GOURMONT, Selections
(translated by Richard Aldington), (1989)

Everyone wants to understand painting.

Why is there no attempt to understand

the song of the birds?

PABLO PICASSO, artist

POINT OF INTEREST

Red deer are among nature's greatest recyclers. There are few waste materials that they do not put to good use. For a start, there's the velvet. This is a blood-rich skin that encourages summer antlergrowth. Once the antler has grown, the velvet rubs off, revealing the sturdy antlers within. Rather than litter the countryside, the stag often eats the discarded velvet for nutrients. The following spring, the dead antler bones drop off, velvet reforms over the stub, and the process begins anew.

In the peat-filled Scottish Highlands, stags gain extra nutrients such as calcium and phosphorus from chewing their discarded antlers. Birthing of young calves begins in late May and continues through to late July, with the majority of calves being born in early to mid-June. After the placenta has been expelled, the hind will eat it and clean any traces of the birth from the area, to minimise the risk of attracting predators.

Still mindful of these predators while suckling her calf, the hind will eat its faeces and urine, to reduce the scent of young deer in the area. This is the most dangerous time: 80% of calf deaths take place in the week after birth.

One crow never pecks out another's eyes.

ANONYMOUS

Then they all went together into the woods, looking everywhere among bushes and brambles to see if they could find the head. And, wonder of wonders, God in his wisdom sent a wolf to watch over the head, and protect it against other wild beasts day and night. The men went about searching, and constantly calling out to one another, as is the custom of woodsmen, 'Where art thou now, my companion?' And the head answered them, saying, 'Here, here, here.' Every time they called the head spoke back to them. There lay the grey wolf watching over the head, with it clasped between his two forepaws. He was greedy and hungry, yet for the sake of God he dared not eat the head but preserved it from other creatures. Then were the men amazed at the wolf's guardianship, and took the holy head away with them, thanking the Almighty for the miracle. And the wolf followed them as they bore away the head, until they came to the town, just as if he were tame, and then returned to the forest.

FROM A 10th CENTURY SAXON DESCRIPTION,
Hunting for the head of their murdered King Edmund

We hope that, when the insects take over the world, they will remember with gratitude how we took them along on all our picnics.

BILL VAUGHAN, journalist

POINT OF INTEREST

Many creatures give off an alarm call as a predator approaches, but it can be important for the other members of their group to know which kind of predator it is they should be fleeing, as the vervet monkey of Africa has worked out. When a vervet monkey sentry sees a leopard it gives a loud bark, the signal to other vervets to leap into the trees where the leopard can't reach. Yet what if the predator is an eagle? The treetops are the worst place to be, so the sentry emits a coughing call, the sign to dash to the ground and hide in a bush. If the predator is a snake, however, then a bush may be a foolish place to hide. A third, sharper call alerts the other vervets to stand on their hind legs to spot the snake for themselves and keep their distance.

The interested friend is a swallow

on the roof.

ANONYMOUS

Do you ever wonder if monkeys have a fear of falling? 30 metres up in the crown of a giant rainforest tree in Borneo, I was once observing young gibbons chasing each other in the branches. I was on an expedition surveying a largely unexplored part of Sarawak near Mount Mulu in northern Borneo. A female gibbon crashed into its brother, missed a handhold and spun out into the abyss, tumbling helplessly towards the forest floor. I was certain it would be injured, but it seemed totally unconcerned. Just above my head, the little female reached out and effortlessly grabbed a passing twig and, in one fluid movement, pulled itself into a tree before racing upwards to the canopy to join its family. It's millions of years since we humans used to be able to do that, and I thought, 'I wish I could do so now'.

ANDREW MITCHELL, The Enchanted Canopy, (1986)

Animals are such agreeable friends – they ask no questions, they pass no criticisms.

GEORGE ELIOT, author

POINT OF INTEREST

The treecreeper is a mouse-like bird that hops its way up the trunks and branches of trees using its long curved bill to pick out insects and larvae from its bark. It's a delightful sight as it hops in a spiral, investigating as it goes, before flying off to try another tree. Then as you're watching it hop along the underside of the branch, you suddenly wonder – why doesn't it fall off? The answer is that as it makes each jump upside-down, it briefly flaps its wings, propelling itself back up to the branch again, although the movement is almost imperceptible.

WILD TALES

My heart is like a singing bird
Whose nest is in a watered shoot;
My heart is like an apple-tree
Whose boughs are bent with thickset fruit;
My heart is like a rainbow shell
That paddles in a halcyon sea;
My heart is gladder than all these
Because my love is come to me.

Raise me a dais of silk and down;
Hang it with vair and purple dyes;
Carve it in doves, and pomegranates,
And peacocks with a hundred eyes;
Work it in gold and silver grapes,
In leaves, and silver fleurs-de-lys;
Because the birthday of my life
Is come, my love is come to me.

CHRISTINA ROSSETTI, A Birthday

PAUSE FOR THOUGHT

The wild creatures I had come to Africa to see are exhilarating in their multitudes and colours, and I imagined for a time that this glimpse of the earth's morning might account for the anticipation that I felt, the sense of origins, of innocence and mystery, like a marvellous childhood faculty restored. Perhaps it is the consciousness that here in Africa, south of the Sahara, our kind was born. But here was also something else that, years ago, under the sky of the Sudan, had made me restless, the stillness in this ancient continent, the echo of so much that has died away, the imminence of so much as yet unknown. Something has happened here, is happening, will happen - whole landscapes seem alert.

PETER MATTHIESSEN, The Tree where Man was Born, (1972)

Before fording the river, do not curse the alligator's mother.

ANONYMOUS

POINT OF INTEREST

Hybridisation between plants is not particularly uncommon, but every now and then one turns up that catches the eye more so than most. In June 1998, a hybrid orchid was discovered, new to Britain, called *Orchiaceras melsheimeri.* Discovered in a Kent woodland, the plant is tall with a cylindrical spike and intermediate flowers. The hoods are crimson, and have tufts of red hairs, while the spur is very small, only about 1mm long. What makes this hybrid so memorable? It was found within a mixed population of its parent plants... the man orchid and the lady orchid.

Genesis begins anew.

It is just like man's vanity and impertinence to call an animal dumb because it is dumb to his dull perceptions.

MARK TWAIN, author

A Fox was mounting a hedge when he lost his footing and caught hold of a Bramble to save himself. Having pricked and grievously worn the soles of his feet, he accused the Bramble because, when he had fled to her for assistance, she had used him worse than the edge itself. The Bramble, interrupting him, said, 'But you really must have been out of your senses to fasten yourself on me, who am myself always accustomed to fasten upon others'.

To the selfish all are selfish.

AESOP, The Fox and the Bramble, Fables, (600 BCE)

Friends tie their purses with a spider's thread.

ANONYMOUS

POINT OF INTEREST

Next time you're in south-east England, take a second look at that bird that's squawking at you from the trees above. The chances are greater than ever before that it's a member of the parrot family, in particular the ring-necked parakeet, that has been slowly developing feral colonies in Greater London, Kent and Sussex, but which has blossomed to a possible population of 4,500 thanks to the hot summer of 2003. There's no doubt that Britain's warmer climes have encouraged the breeding success of this bird (can anyone still be in serious doubt about global warming?), but where did it come from in the first place? The most accepted belief is that a few broke out from private collections some 20-30 years ago, although more fascinating theories include the idea that some might have hitched a ride on the undercarriage of a London-bound jet (hence their prevalence in Richmond Park), or that today's entire

population may have resulted from a pair that escaped during the filming of *The African Queen* at Shepperton Studios, starring Humphrey Bogart, Katherine Hepburn, and some parakeets.

The greatness of a nation and its moral progress can be judged by the way its animals are treated.

MAHATMA GANDHI, statesman

Let me evoke the hawkmoths, the jets of my boyhood! Colours would die a long death on June evenings. The lilac shrubs in full bloom before which I stood, net in hand, displayed clusters of a fluffy grey in the dusk – the ghost of purple. A moist young moon hung above the mist of a neighbouring meadow... And suddenly it would come, the low buzz passing from flower to flower, the vibrational halo around the streamlined body of an olive and pink hummingbird hawk-moth poised in the air above the corolla into which it had dipped its long tongue. Its handsome black larva (resembling a diminutive cobra when it puffed out its ocellated front segments) could be found on dank willow herb two months later. Thus, every hour and season had its delights. And, finally, on cold, or even frosty, autumn nights, one could sugar for months by painting tree trunks with a mixture of molasses, beer, and rum. Through the gusty blackness, one's lantern would illumine the stickily glistening furrows of the bark and two or three large moths upon it imbibing the sweets, their nervous wings half open butterfly fashion, the lower ones exhibiting their incredible crimson silk from beneath the lichen-grey primaries. '*Catocala adultera!*' I would triumphantly shriek in the direction of the lighted windows of the house as I stumbled home to show my captures to my father.

VLADIMIR NABOKOV, Speak, Memory: An Autobiography Revisited, (1951)

It's better to feed one cat than many birds.

SCANDINAVIAN PROVERB

POINT OF INTEREST

For centuries, the barnacle goose was thought to be a fish. This was because the bird, which graces Europe in the winter, flies off to the Arctic to breed in the summer. As people had no idea where it went, and never saw either eggs or goslings, they assumed it must be the offspring of creatures often found near its watery habitat, i.e. barnacles. Believing the goose grew within large bivalves until mature, they reasoned it was a fish, thus allowing Catholics to eat it on Fridays. The belief existed in many areas until the 18th century: one species of barnacle is even named *Lepas anatifera* – 'goose-bringer' – a title bestowed by Linnaeus in 1767.

When the eagles are silent, the parrots begin to jabber.

SIR WINSTON CHURCHILL, politician

A Raven saw a Swan and desired to secure for himself the same beautiful plumage. Supposing that the Swan's splendid white colour rose from his washing in the water in which he swam, the Raven left the altars in the neighbourhood where he picked up his living, and took up residence in the lakes and pools. But cleansing his feathers as often as he would, he could not change their colour, while through want of food he perished.

Change of habit cannot alter nature.

AESOP, The Raven and the Swan, Fables, (600 BCE)

A hen is only an egg's way of making another egg.

SAMUEL BUTLER, author

POINT OF INTEREST

When Madagascar split away from Africa 165
million years ago, its flora and fauna evolved quite
independently from that of the mainland. Lemurs
are the best-known example of creatures that are
endemic to the island, but the largest lemur of all is
the most extraordinary. The indri, reasonably common
until a century ago, but now numbering only a few
thousand individuals, weighs up to 22lb and only
comes down to the ground to cross treeless areas, or
sometimes to eat dirt. Giving birth only once every
two or three years, the indri emits an eerie call that
sounds human in tone, and is picked up by other indri
through the rainforest, surrounding the listener with
wailing, child-like howls.

Unsurprisingly, many legends exist in Madagascar
relating to indris giving birth to human children.
Incidentally, the animal gets its name from the

Malagasy for 'Look at that', which is what the first arriving Europeans were told when the lemur was pointed out to them.

His imagination resembled the wings of an ostrich. It enabled him to run, though not to soar.

BARON MACAULEY, historian and politician, on poet John Dryden

As he sat on the grass and looked across the river, a dark hole in the bank opposite, just above the water's edge, caught his eye, and dreamily he fell to considering what a nice snug dwelling-place it would make for an animal with few wants and fond of a bijou riverside residence, above flood level and remote from noise and dust. As he gazed, something bright and small seemed to twinkle down in the heart of it, vanished, then twinkled once more like a tiny star. But it could hardly be a star in such an unlikely situation; and it was too glittering and small for a glow-worm. Then, as he looked, it winked at him, and so declared itself to be an eye; and a small face began gradually to grow up round it, like a frame round a picture. A brown little face, with whiskers. A grave round face, with the same twinkle in its eye that had first attracted his notice. Small neat ears and thick silky hair. It was the Water Rat!

KENNETH GRAHAME, The Wind in the Willows, (1905)

For the strength of the Pack is the Wolf

and the strength of the Wolf, the Pack

RUDYARD KIPLING, author

POINT OF INTEREST

The skink bears its young live, but unlike other live-bearing creatures, the sex of the young is determined by the temperature in which the pregnant female lives. The warmer the environment, the more likely the offspring are to be male, up to about 32°C, at which not a single female is born.

Living as it does in alpine areas, the water skink's habitat temperature is therefore at just the right balance to produce the optimum percentage of male and female young. Yet if predictions are correct, and the region warms up in the coming decades, then the female water skink may become a thing of the past... as would the species.

UNTAMED LANDSCAPES

I wandered lonely as a cloud
That floats on high o'er vales and hills,
When all at once I saw a crowd,
A host, of golden daffodils;
Beside the lake, beneath the trees,
Fluttering and dancing in the breeze.

Continuous as the stars that shine
And twinkle on the milky way,
They stretched in never-ending line
Along the margin of a bay:
Ten thousand saw I at a glance,
Tossing their heads in sprightly dance.

The waves beside them danced; but they
Out-did the sparkling waves in glee:
A poet could not but be gay,
In such a jocund company:
I gazed—and gazed—but little thought
What wealth the show to me had brought:

For oft, when on my couch I lie
In vacant or in pensive mood,
They flash upon that inward eye
Which is the bliss of solitude;
And then my heart with pleasure fills,
And dances with the daffodils.

WILLIAM WORDSWORTH,
I Wandered Lonely as a Cloud

In that green country with its cool deep valleys and fantastic rocks, the narrow paths wind over the hills, linking village to hamlet; they cross streams and wander through woods with ancient names, a thousand intersecting paths, which have been used by the countryman from Saxon times. From the highest parts one can trace the grass-covered roads, along which no cart travels. There are curling hedges which hold protecting arms round odd little fields, and dark lichened stone walls cutting and dividing the green, and everywhere there are woods, beech woods, a flaming fire in the back end of the year, soft as clouds in spring, oak woods, rough and sturdy, plantations of dark fir and tender larch, and mixed woods of many colours and sounds, sheltering fox and badger, woods full of enchantment.

ALISON UTTLEY, Country World, (1984)

Everything is blooming most recklessly;

if it were voices instead of colours, there

would be an unbelievable shrieking into

the heart of the night.

RAINER MARIA RILKE, poet

POINT OF INTEREST

Until recently, little was known about life in tropical forest treetops, because getting up there was nearly impossible. Early explorers used ropes and pulleys or ladders carved into tree trunks. Today, biologists explore the canopy via towers, suspension bridges, rafts lowered gently onto treetops by dirigibles, and even construction cranes. We now know that about 90% of all organisms in a rainforest are found in the canopy. The sun that barely reaches the forest floor strikes treetops with full force, fuelling the photosynthesis that results in leaves, fruit, and seeds. Since there's so much good food way up there, animals abound in the canopy.

For example, a study of rainforest canopy in Peru with 500 cubic metres of foliage (about the size of a two-car garage) found more than 50 species of ants,

1,000 beetle species, 1,700 arthropod species, and more than 100,000 individuals. A rainforest tree alone can have some 1,200 species of beetle, while a single hectare of rich forest canopy is projected to have 12,448 beetle species.

There is nothing in which the birds differ more from man than the way in which they can build and yet leave a landscape as it was before.

ROBERT LYND, sociologist

The wise man will never weary of looking at green grass and green trees. It is an unspeakable refreshment to the eye and the mind: and the daily pressure of occupation cannot touch one here. One wonders that human beings who always live amid such scenery do not look more like it. But some people are utterly unimpressionable by the influences of outward scenery. You may know men who have lived for many years where Nature has done her best with wood and rock and river: and even when you become well acquainted with them, you cannot discover the faintest trace in their talk or in their feeling of the mightily powerful touch (as it would be to so many) which has been unceasingly laid upon them through all that time. Or you may have beheld a vacuous person at a picnic party, who amid traces of God's handiwork that should make men hold their breath, does but pass from the occupation of fatuously flirting with a young woman like himself, to furiously abusing the servants for not sufficiently cooling the wine... A human being ought to be very thankful if his disposition be such that he heartily enjoys green grass and green trees.

ANDREW KENNEDY HUTCHISON BOYD,
Autumn Holidays of a Country Parson, (1865)

I do not know what I may appear to the world; but to myself I seem to have been only like a boy playing on the seashore, and diverting myself in now and then finding a smoother pebble or a prettier shell than ordinary, whilst the great ocean of truth lay all undiscovered before me.

ISAAC NEWTON, scientist

POINT OF INTEREST

The Isles of Scilly are like nowhere else in the world: a microcosm of diversity, a unique way of life, and a beautiful, unspoilt natural environment. Auks, petrels, shearwaters and fulmars breed around the archipelago, while bats, which do not hibernate due to the warm climate, can be seen feeding all year round.

The sea life is, of course, impressive. Porpoises, dolphins and the occasional whale are to be looked out for, along with the spectacular sun fish, easily seen as the water is so clear around the islands. Landbased mammals are few and far between, but the eastern isles are very good for seals, and if you're very lucky, you might catch a glimpse of the endemic Scilly shrew. The heady scent of the narcissus crop fills the winter air, while three types of adder's-tongue fern grace St Agnes Island. The four inhabited islands can be explored via a series of permissive paths, and the whole natural spectacle is looked after by The Isles of Scilly Wildlife Trust.

No-one else seems to have seen the sparkle on the brook, or heard the music at the hatch, or to have felt back through the centuries; and when I try to describe these things to them they look at me with stolid incredulity. No-one seems to understand how I get food from the clouds, nor what there was in the night, nor why it is not so good to look at it out of a window.

RICHARD JEFFERIES, naturalist and poet

When he reached the place he was aiming for, he began making holes in the ground with his rod, putting an acorn in each and then covering it up again. He was planting oak trees. I asked him if the land was his. He said it wasn't. Did he know who the owner was? No, he didn't. He thought it must be common land, or perhaps it belonged to people who weren't interested in it. He wasn't interested in who they were. And so, with great care, he planted his hundred acorns. After the midday meal he started sorting out more acorns to sow. I must have been very pressing with my questions, because he answered them. He'd been planting trees in this wilderness for three years. He'd planted a hundred thousand of them. Out of those, twenty thousand had come up. Of the twenty thousand he expected to lose half, because of rodents or the unpredictable ways of Providence. That still meant ten thousand oaks would grow where before there had been nothing. It was at this point that I wondered how old he was. He was obviously over fifty. Fifty-five, he said. His name was Elzéard Bouffier. He had once owned a farm on the plains. It was there he had lived his life. But he had lost first his only son, then his wife. After that he came here to be alone, enjoying an unhurried existence with his sheep and his dog.

But it struck him that this part of the country was dying for lack of trees, and having nothing much else to do he decided to put things right.

JEAN GIONO, The Man who Planted Trees, (1953)

The Creator has an inordinate fondness for beetles.

JBS HALDANE, naturalist

POINT OF INTEREST

Ancient woods are those where there is believed to have been continuous woodland cover since at least 1600 AD. Before this planting was uncommon, so a wood present in 1600 AD was likely to have developed naturally. In Scotland, ancient woodland sites are strictly those shown as semi-natural woodland on the 'Roy' maps (a 1750 military survey and the best source of historical map evidence), and as woodland on all subsequent maps, however they have been combined with long-established woods of semi-natural origin (originating from between 1750 and 1860) into a single category of ancient woodland to take account of uncertainties in compilation of the ancient woodland inventory. Ancient semi-natural woodland (ASNW) is composed of native tree species that have not obviously been planted. Planted ancient woodland sites (PAWS) are ancient woods in which the former tree cover has been replaced,

often with non-native trees. Important features of ancient woodland often survive in many of these woods, including characteristic flora and fauna, and archaeology. Our remaining ancient woodland covers less than 2% of the UK, and is irreplaceable.

In the ant's house, dew is a deluge.

ANONYMOUS

I often pulled my hat over my eyes to watch the rising of the lark, or to see the hawk hang in the summer sky and the kite take its circles round the wood. I often lingered a minute on the woodland stile to hear the woodpigeons clapping their wings among the dark oaks. I hunted curious flowers in rapture and muttered thoughts in their praise. I loved the pasture with its rushes and thistles and sheep-tracks. I adored the wild, marshy fen with its solitary heronshaw sweeping along in its melancholy sky. I wandered the heath in raptures among the rabbit burrows and golden-blossomed furze. I dropt down on a thymy molehill or mossy eminence to survey the summer landscape... I marked the various colours in flat, spreading fields, checkered into closes of different-tinctured grain like the colours of a map; the copper-tinted clover in blossom; the sun-tanned green of the ripening hay; the lighter charlock and the sunset imitation of the scarlet headaches; the blue corn-bottles crowding their splendid colours in large sheets over the land and troubling the cornfields with destroying beauty; the different greens of the woodland trees, the dark oak, the paler ash, the mellow lime, the white poplars peeping above the rest like leafy steeples, the grey willow shining in the sun, as if the morning mist still lingered on its cool green... I observed all this with the same raptures as I have done since. But I knew nothing of poetry. It was felt and not uttered.

JOHN CLARE, The Autobiography

I want meadows red in tone and trees painted in blue. Nature has no imagination.

CHARLES BAUDELAIRE, poet

POINT OF INTEREST

Sometimes an entire island can become a naturalists' paradise, and the Isle of Eigg, of the Inner Hebrides, is no exception. Accessing the island by ferry, visitors have a reasonable chance of watching minke whales as they cross between the months of July and September. Once on the island itself, wildflower meadows, hazel woods and heather moors open up, while the craggy outline plays host to eagles. This is one of the great joys of the island: so many habitats within such close walking distance of each other. The bird list is just short of 200 species – impressive for such a small isle – and the plantlife is rich, including 12 species of orchid and 20 nationally rare bryophytes. With otters, 18 species of butterfly, the pygmy shrew and the island wood mouse, brought over by the Norse raiders, Eigg, now co-managed by the Scottish Wildlife Trust, offers a stunning variety of sights and discoveries.

Only the nightingale can understand

the rose.

ANONYMOUS

Our ancestors, most of whom lived all the year round in unadulterated rural surroundings, took less conscious note of natural beauty, because it was the common air they breathed, the element in which they lived and moved. It pervaded and formed their finds and personalities. The Cavaliers drew their charm from the fields and the Roundheads their strength from the earth. Cavalier and Roundhead are alike a vanished race, for they are not to be bred under the influences of modern city life, machinery and the cheap press of today. So, too, it was the influence of the fields and woods of Elizabethan England that fostered the thousand-and-one lyric poets and musicians, those 'bards who died content on pleasant sward, leaving great verse unto a little clan'.

GM TREVELYAN, An Autobiography and Other Essays, (1949)

And thus, our life, exempt from public haunt, finds tongues in trees, books in the running brooks, sermons in stones, and good in everything.

WILLIAM SHAKESPEAERE, playwright

POINT OF INTEREST

The cliffs of South Gower near Port Eynon in Wales is one of the great coastal havens of Britain. A mixture of habitats merge here, from limestone grassland and scree to maritime heath, rocky foreshore and caves to relict sand dune grassland. It's the only site anywhere in Britain where yellow whitlow grass grows, while the silky wave moth is one of its flagship species. Sea-watching can barely be matched, here, either, with rare birds recorded every year, while raven, chough and Dartford warbler feature inland.

It's an impressive feeling to stand high on the cliffs knowing that ancient life once inhabited the rocks below. A medieval dovecote was built into the cliffs in more recent times, but the caves, which were inhabited 30,000 years ago, are some of the richest Upper Paleolithic prehistoric sites in Britain.

TRIGGER™
The mental health & wellbeing publisher

We want to help you to not just survive but thrive ... one book at a time

Find out more about Trigger Publishing by visiting our website:

triggerpublishing.com

or join us on:

Twitter @**TriggerPub**

Facebook @**TriggerPub**

Instagram @**TriggerPub**

*Shaw*mind
Your Local Mental Health & Wellbeing Charity

A proportion of profits from the sale of all Trigger books

go to their sister charity Shaw Mind,

founded by Adam Shaw and Lauren Callaghan.

The charity aims to ensure that everyone has access

to mental health resources whenever they need them.

Find out more: **shawmindfoundation.org**

or join them on:

Twitter: @**Shaw_Mind**

Instagram: @**Shaw_Mind**

LinkedIn: @**shaw-mind**

FB: @**shawmindUK**